MAZES
"MY KIDS LOVE 'EM!"

BY JD PUZZLE BOOKS

Mazes: "My kids love 'em!"
by JD Puzzle Books

HAVE FUN!

EASY!

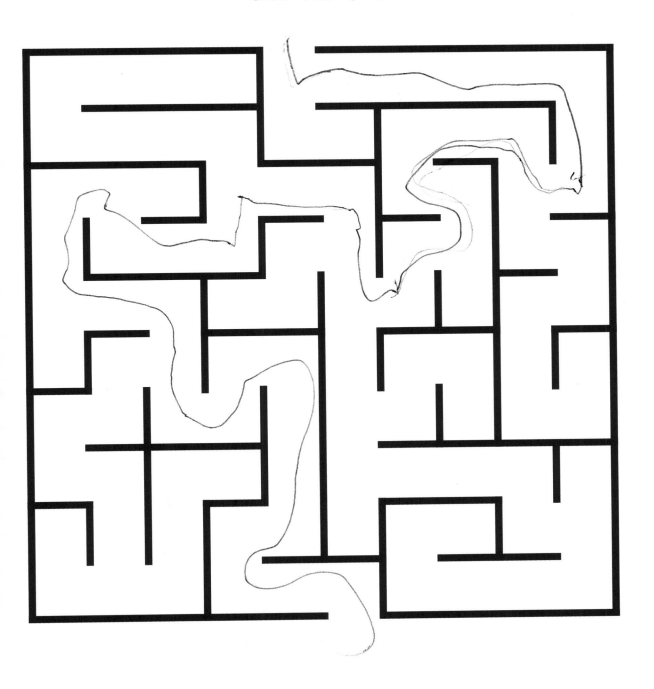

SOLUTION

EASY!

SOLUTION

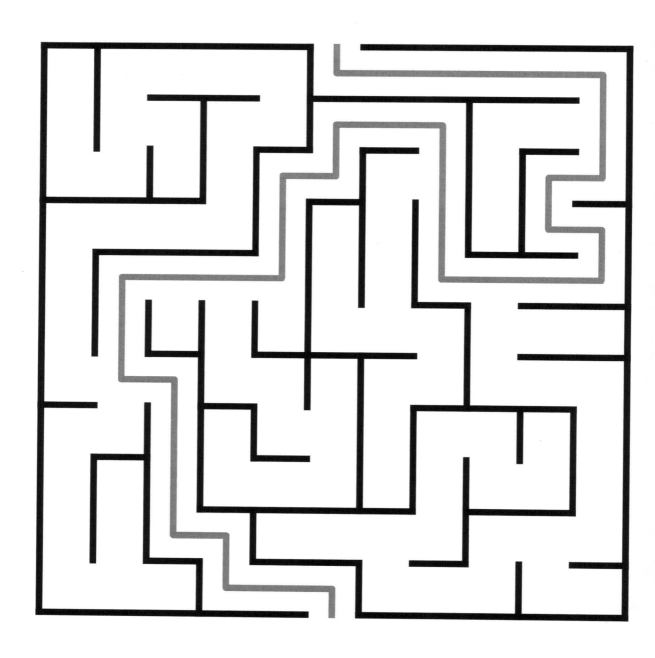

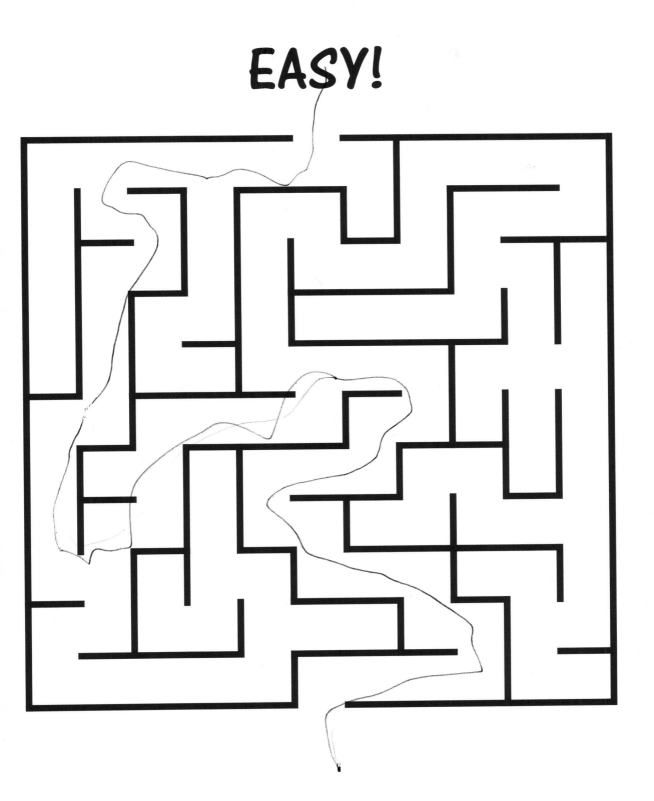

SOLUTION

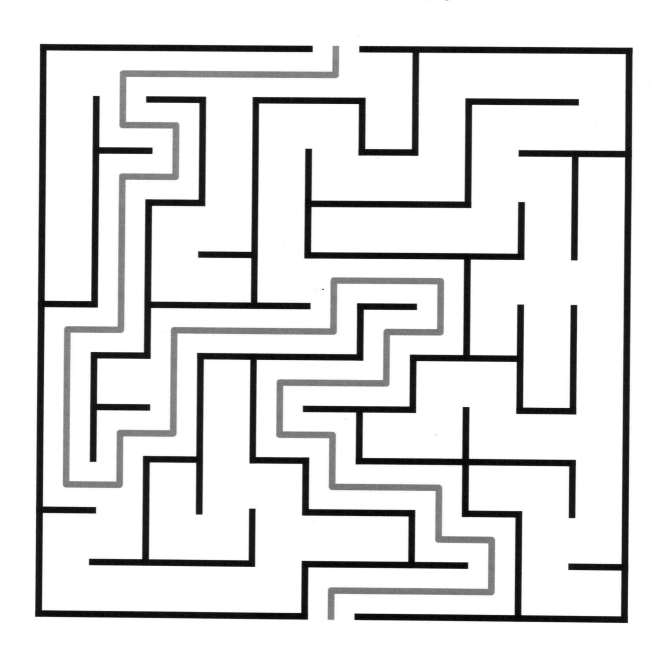

SOLUTION

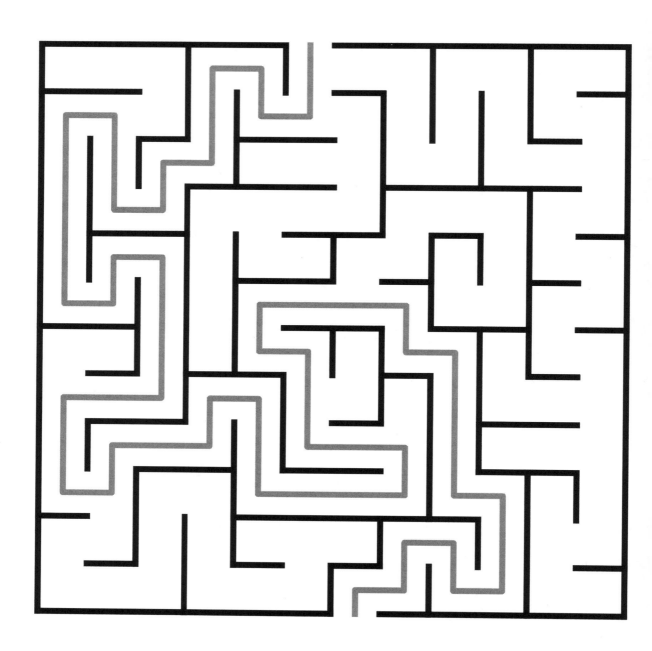

EASY!

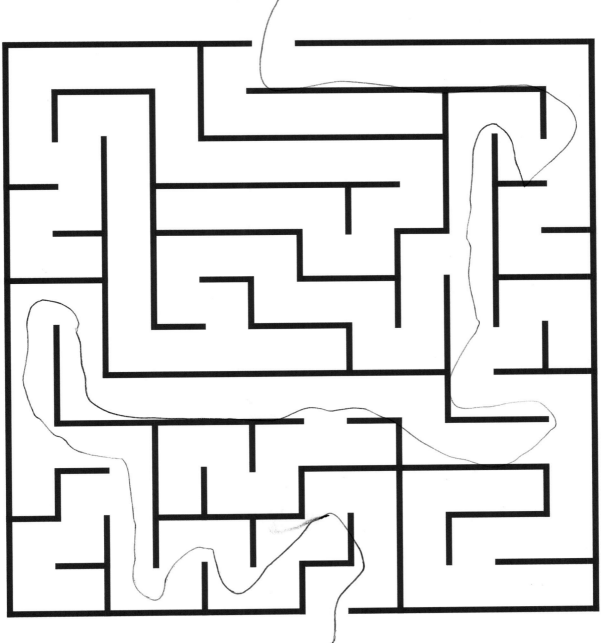

SOLUTION

EASY!

SOLUTION

EASY!

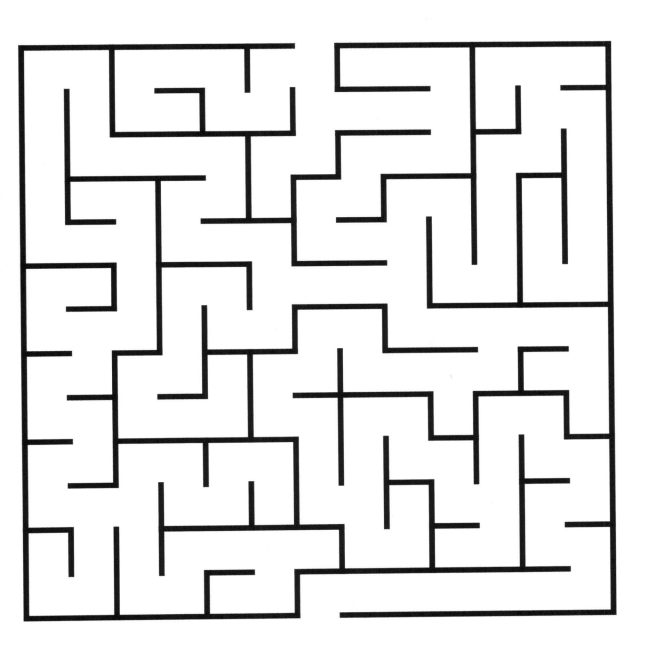

SOLUTION

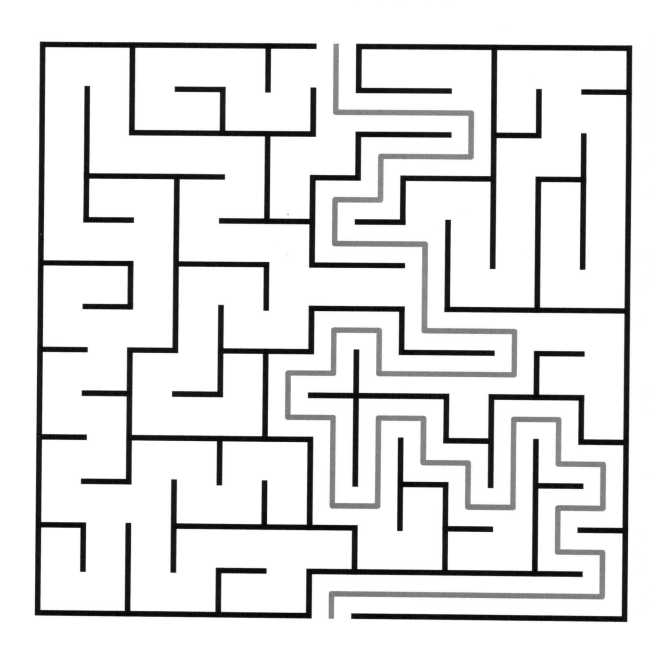

EASY!

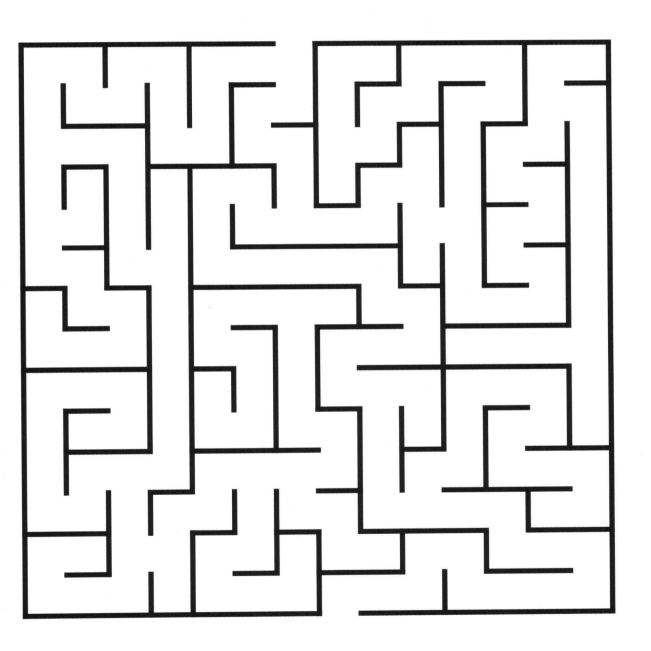

SOLUTION

EASY!

SOLUTION

GETTING TRICKY!

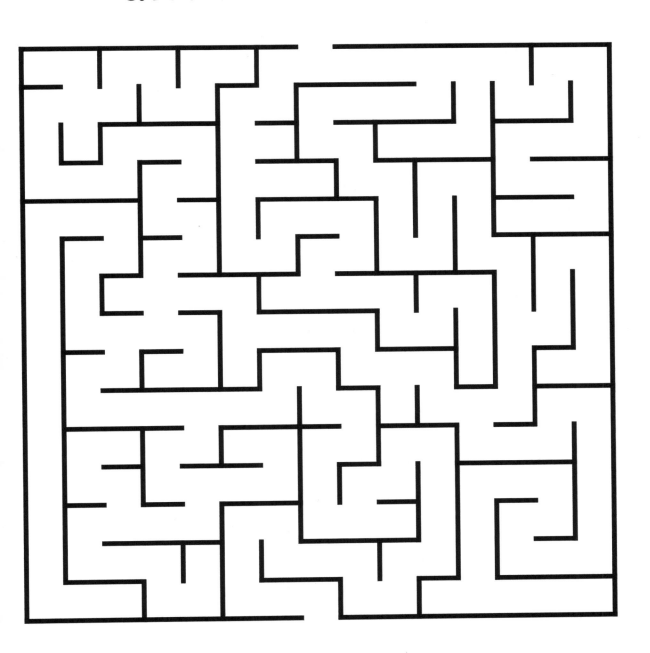

SOLUTION

GETTING TRICKY!

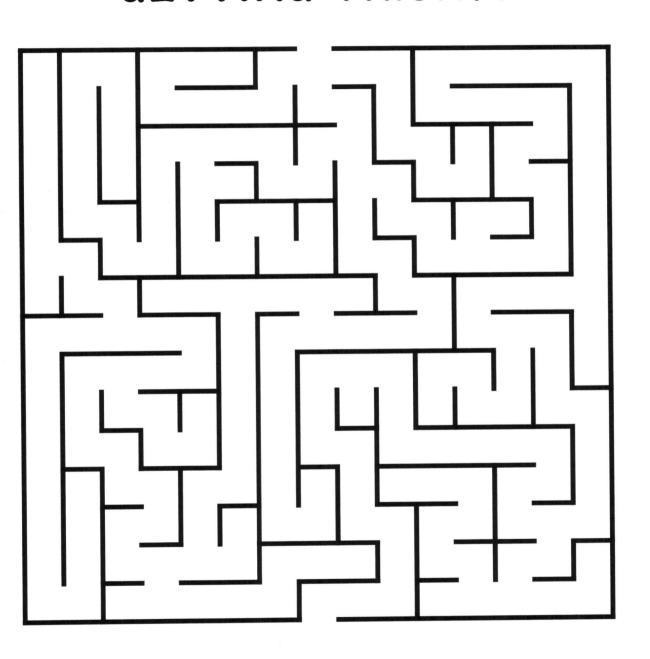

SOLUTION

GETTING TRICKY!

SOLUTION

GETTING TRICKY!

SOLUTION

GETTING TRICKY!

SOLUTION

GETTING TRICKY!

SOLUTION

GETTING TRICKY!

SOLUTION

GETTING TRICKY!

SOLUTION

GETTING TRICKY!

SOLUTION

GETTING TRICKY!

SOLUTION

GETTING TRICKY!

SOLUTION

GETTING TRICKY!

SOLUTION

GETTING TRICKY!

SOLUTION

GETTING TRICKY!

SOLUTION

TRICKY!

SOLUTION

TRICKY!

SOLUTION

TRICKY!

SOLUTION

TRICKY!

SOLUTION

TRICKY!

SOLUTION

TRICKY!

SOLUTION

TRICKY!

SOLUTION

TRICKY!

SOLUTION

TRICKY!

SOLUTION

TRICKY!

SOLUTION

TRICKY!

SOLUTION

TRICKY!

SOLUTION

TRICKY!

SOLUTION

TRICKY!

SOLUTION

YOU'RE A PRO!

SOLUTION

YOU'RE A PRO!

SOLUTION

YOU'RE A PRO!

SOLUTION

YOU'RE A PRO!

SOLUTION

YOU'RE A PRO!

SOLUTION

YOU'RE A PRO!

SOLUTION

YOU'RE A PRO!

SOLUTION

YOU'RE A PRO!

SOLUTION

YOU'RE A PRO!

SOLUTION

YOU'RE A PRO!

SOLUTION

YOU'RE A PRO!

SOLUTION

YOU'RE A PRO!

SOLUTION

YOU'RE A PRO!

SOLUTION

YOU'RE A PRO!

SOLUTION

YOU'RE A MASTER!

SOLUTION

YOU'RE A MASTER!

SOLUTION

YOU'RE A MASTER!

SOLUTION

YOU'RE A MASTER!

SOLUTION

YOU'RE A MASTER!

SOLUTION

YOU'RE A MASTER!

SOLUTION

YOU'RE A MASTER!

SOLUTION

YOU'RE A MASTER!

SOLUTION

YOU'RE A MASTER!

SOLUTION

27798132R00073

Made in the USA
Middletown, DE
21 December 2015